GREAT PREDATORS

CROCODILE

by Tammy Gagne

Content Consultant
Martha L. (Marty) Crump
Adjunct Professor
Department of Biology
Utah State University

CORE
LIBRARY

Published by ABDO Publishing Company, PO Box 398166, Minneapolis, MN 55439. Copyright © 2014 by Abdo Consulting Group, Inc. International copyrights reserved in all countries. No part of this book may be reproduced in any form without written permission from the publisher. The Core Library™ is a trademark and logo of ABDO Publishing Company.

Printed in the United States of America,
North Mankato, Minnesota
052013
092013
♻ THIS BOOK CONTAINS AT LEAST 10% RECYCLED MATERIALS.

Editor: Lauren Coss
Series Designer: Becky Daum

Library of Congress Control Number: 2013932510

Cataloging-in-Publication Data
Gagne, Tammy.
 Crocodile / Tammy Gagne.
  p. cm. -- (Great Predators)
 ISBN 978-1-61783-946-7 (lib. bdg.)
 ISBN 978-1-62403-011-6 (pbk.)
 Includes bibliographical references and index.
 1. Crocodiles--Juvenile literature. 2. Predatory animals--Juvenile literature.
 I. Title.
 597.98--dc23

                                    2013932510

Photo Credits: Roxana Gonzalez/Shutterstock Images, cover, 1; David Acosta Allely/Shutterstock Images, 4; Shutterstock Images, 7 (top; second from top), 7 (middle; bottom), 7 (second from bottom), 10, 12, 40; Jupiter Images/Thinkstock, 8; Biosphoto/SuperStock, 15; Wilfredo Lee/AP Images, 17; Animals Animals/SuperStock, 18; Trevor Kelly/Shutterstock Images, 20; Sergey Uryadnikov/Shutterstock Images, 23; Andre Anita/Shutterstock Images, 24, 43; World's Wildlife Wonders/Shutterstock Images, 26; Belinda Images/SuperStock, 28; Red Line Editorial, 32; Thinkstock, 33, 45; Andre Maritz/Shutterstock Images, 34; iStockphoto, 37; Discovery Networks US/AP Images, 39

CONTENTS

CHAPTER ONE

THE MIGHTY CROCODILE

A group of lions stands quietly near the Nile River. They are watching a young water buffalo drink from a watering hole. The lions are waiting for the right time to attack. Before they have the chance, a crocodile seems to come out of nowhere. It lunges out of the water, snapping its strong jaws around the helpless animal. The water buffalo doesn't stand a chance against the powerful

Nile crocodiles are some of the largest crocodiles in the world.

Prehistoric Super Croc

In 2001 the remains of a giant prehistoric crocodile were found in the Sahara Desert. The beast was 39 feet (12 m) long. It probably weighed more than nine tons (8.2 metric tons). The skull alone measured more than six and one-half feet (2 m). This is longer than an average person. According to paleontologists, this distant relative to the modern crocodile lived 110 million years ago. It ate large dinosaurs.

predator. The reptile had been lurking in the water the whole time. It waited for the right moment to make its move. The lions retreat. They will have to find another meal today.

Crocs Big and Small

Twenty-three different species of crocodiles live in the world today. The biggest of these is the saltwater crocodile, nicknamed the saltie. Some salties grow as long as 23 feet (7 m). They can weigh as much as 2,200 pounds (1,000 kg). Most members of this species are slightly smaller. They measure approximately 17 feet (5 m) long and weigh

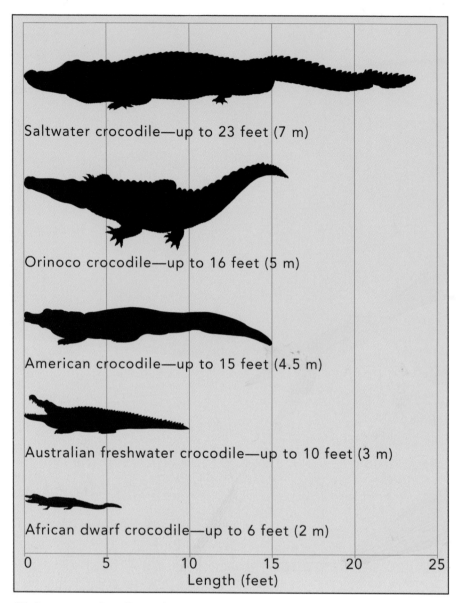

Saltwater crocodile—up to 23 feet (7 m)

Orinoco crocodile—up to 16 feet (5 m)

American crocodile—up to 15 feet (4.5 m)

Australian freshwater crocodile—up to 10 feet (3 m)

African dwarf crocodile—up to 6 feet (2 m)

0   5   10   15   20   25

Length (feet)

Sizing up the Species

All crocodiles are not the same. One of the most obvious differences between the species is size. This chart shows the sizes of a few well-known crocodile species. Is the size difference bigger or smaller than you imagined after reading about crocodile sizes? How might the size of a croc change the way it lives and hunts in the wild?

Dwarf crocodiles are much smaller than other crocodile species.

approximately 1,000 pounds (450 kg). Even these saltwater crocs are about four times bigger than an average person.

The smallest known crocodiles are African dwarf crocodiles. They grow to only five feet long (1.5 m). One species of African dwarf crocodile was discovered in West Africa so recently that it hasn't been named yet.

A Rough Exterior

At first glance a croc looks like an oversized lizard. It has a long body and tail, short legs, and a pointed snout. Crocodiles may be grayish green or dark brown in color. These earthy tones help camouflage the animals. American crocodiles have dark stripes on their bodies and tails when they are young. As they get older, the stripes remain on their tails only.

A crocodile's body is covered with scales. These rough plates of

Crocodile Cousins

Crocodiles belong to an order of reptiles called *Crocodylia*. Alligators, caimans, and other large reptiles also belong to this order. Crocodiles belong to the *Crocodylidae* family. Alligators and caimans belong to the *Alligatoridae* family. The Indian gharial is the only member of the third Crocodylia family, the *Gavialidae* family. Of these reptiles, alligators and crocs look the most alike. The quickest way to tell an alligator from a crocodile is by comparing the animals' snouts. A crocodile's jaw is v-shaped. An alligator's snout is more rounded. It looks like the letter *u*.

9

Crocodiles tear chunks of meat off their prey when eating.

hardened skin act like body armor. They protect the animal from other predators. Crocodile scales fall off one at a time. Then new scales grow in to take their places.

Crocodiles also lose and replace their teeth throughout their lives. When one tooth falls out, another grows into the same spot. Crocs do not use their teeth to chew their food. Instead they use them to grab on to their prey. Once they have a firm grip, the reptiles roll with the prey in the water. Crocs use this technique to drown their prey. This also helps the crocodiles tear chunks of meat off the animal. They swallow these big chunks of meat whole.

Crocs are powerful predators that grow up to be very big. But they start out very small.

CHAPTER TWO

LONG LIVE THE CROCODILE

Even experts aren't certain exactly how long crocodiles live. Scientists have studied wild crocs between 30 and 70 years of age. The smaller species are more likely to live 30 to 50 years. The larger ones have been known to live 50 to 70 years. Some crocodiles have even outlived the scientists studying them.

All crocodiles hatch from eggs.

A Long, Long Life

One of the oldest known crocodiles lived in a zoo in Yekaterinburg, Russia. The croc was named Kolya. He was 9 feet, 10 inches (3 m) long when he died in 1995. He was thought to be between 110 and 115 years old when he died. During Kolya's lifetime, Russia endured two world wars and a revolution.

Finding a Mate

Both male and female crocs are ready to mate when they are about ten years old. But mating age can vary by species. When a female crocodile is ready to mate, she will swim to the surface of the water and growl. She will also give off a special scent. Both the noise and the odor attract male crocs in the area. Once the female has chosen a mate, the pair will spend a lot of time together. They may stay together for months.

Baby Crocodiles

Crocodile mating seasons and habits vary by species. Saltwater crocs usually mate between November and March. Females often make nests out of grass beside the water or dig holes for their eggs. A single female

A female Nile crocodile guards her nest.

croc can lay between 25 and 90 eggs at one time. The eggs take up to 90 days to hatch.

For some croc species, such as Cuban crocodiles, the temperature inside the nest determines the gender of the babies. Temperatures between 89.6 and 91.4 degrees Fahrenheit (32°–33°C) produce male crocs. Temperatures higher or lower than this range produce females.

Some mother crocs stay close to their nests to guard the eggs. Other animals, including the father

Telling a Crocodile's Age

At one time scientists looked to crocodiles' bones to find out their age. Growth rings develop in their bones over time. This method isn't very specific. Many scientists now capture young wild crocodiles to study them. They mark these young crocs with microchips before releasing them. The scientists collect more information if the animals are recaptured. They can guess the animal's age by counting backward to the date they placed the microchip.

crocodile, often try to eat the eggs. But these predators are unlikely to succeed when the protective mother is nearby.

A baby crocodile's teeth start growing even before it hatches. The baby has a special tooth on the end of its snout. This tooth is called an egg tooth. The baby uses this tooth to tear its way out of the egg. Some baby crocodiles make barking sounds when they are ready to be born. Mothers often respond by biting at the eggs gently. They help break the shells so their babies can escape. Baby crocs are called hatchlings once they leave their shells.

Researchers put microchips in newborn crocs to monitor the reptiles as they grow up.

Female crocodiles can be gentle mothers. As soon as the hatchlings leave their eggs, some mothers carry them in their mouths to the water. In some species, the mother guards the hatchlings for most of the first year of their lives. Most one-year-old crocodiles are able to care for themselves. Eventually each croc sets out to find a habitat of its own.

Daily Lives

Crocodiles are nocturnal. This means that they are most active during the night. Most crocs nap in the sun during the day. But they don't sleep as soundly

Nile crocodile females are known for carrying their hatchlings in their mouths.

as people do. The smallest noise or movement will wake them.

Adult crocodiles are fairly social animals. Females often play together, chasing one another in the water. Male Nile crocodiles work together to roll heavy prey. Saltwater crocs are far less friendly when it comes to food. They would rather fight each other than share a kill.

Baby crocodiles can communicate with their mothers as well as with each other. In 2008 the United Kingdom newspaper the *Telegraph* reported on how French scientists researched the baby crocs' conversations:

> *French scientists Amelie Vergne and Nicolas Mathevon of Université Jean Monnet in Saint-Etienne noticed that the young reptiles make a noise, described as sounding like "umph, umph," in the moments immediately before they hatch. The researchers tested ten batches of crocodile eggs, dividing them into three groups. One was played actual recordings of the juveniles' pre-hatching calls, one was played random noises, and one was left in silence. Eggs played the real recordings all hatched within ten minutes, while the other two groups stayed in their shells for another five hours at least.*

Source: Tom Chivers and Agencies. "Baby Crocodiles Talk to Each Other in Their Eggs." Telegraph. Telegraph Media Group, June 24, 2008. Web. Accessed March 21, 2013.

Back It Up

Read this passage carefully. The author is using evidence to support a point. Write a short paragraph describing the point the author is making. Then write down two or three key pieces of evidence the author uses to support this main point.

CHAPTER THREE

PATIENT PREDATORS

Crocodiles are semi-aquatic reptiles. This means that they live both on land and in water. What a crocodile eats depends on where it lives. Nearly all crocs eat fish. But they will also eat larger animals if they are available. A crocodile can eat half its own body weight at one time. In Africa crocs will eat carrion, or the remains of dead animals. African crocs will also dine on small hippos and zebras. In Australia

A hungry crocodile snatches a bird from the air.

Jumping Crocs

Crocodiles can jump surprisingly high and fast. In less than one second, these animals can move several feet in the air. If you see a croc raise its head, it may be getting ready to jump toward whatever is above it. Many crocs catch birds this way. Crocs are very good at judging distance. If they can see their prey, chances are good that they can catch it by jumping.

crocs will eat dingoes, kangaroos, and wallabies. American crocodiles eat birds, crabs, and turtles.

Crocodiles are strong swimmers. They can reach a top speed of up to 18 miles per hour (29 km/h) in water. But they cannot swim at this pace for long. A more normal speed for crocs is two to three miles per hour (3–5 km/h). A crocodile uses its tail to propel itself through the water. On land crocs can run approximately seven miles per hour (11 km/h). At this speed they can often outrun a human.

Most crocodiles hunt by themselves. Even though they can move quickly, crocs don't usually chase their prey. They would rather wait for prey to come to

Even large crocs, like this Cuban crocodile, can jump high out of the water.

Crocodiles are strong enough to drag a large animal, such as a wildebeest, into the water.

them. When an animal comes near, a croc lunges at it. Because a crocodile is normally so still, this sudden movement almost always catches the prey by surprise.

The American crocodile attracts prey with a clever trick. The croc throws up a small bit of food. This lures live fish into the area. When these fish get close to the food, the hungry croc snaps them up in its jaws.

Powerful Jaws

Saltwater crocodiles have one of the strongest bites for their size of any living animal. Opening a crocodile's mouth after it is closed is nearly impossible. However, keeping a croc's jaws closed is extremely easy. The muscles that allow a croc to open its mouth are very weak. A human's hand is strong enough to keep a crocodile's mouth closed.

Crocs are cold-blooded. They use the heat from their environment to stay warm. They do not depend on the energy they get from food to

Crocodile Tears

In ancient times people believed that crocodiles cried to lure prey to them. Smaller animals were said to come closer when they saw a croc weeping. The sly croc would then snap them up with its powerful jaws. Crocodiles do release tears when they eat. Scientists think that this happens due to the large amounts of air that the animals blow out as they feed. This also empties the crocs' tear glands. People are said to cry crocodile tears when they are pretending to be sad over something.

Crocodiles have very strong jaws. Once a croc bites down, its prey is unlikely to escape.

warm their bodies. Because of this, crocodiles can go an entire year without eating. However, few crocs actually go a full year without eating. Most eat about 50 times each year.

Both alligators and crocodiles have thousands of tiny black bumps on their heads and jaws. For a long time no one knew exactly what these little domes did. In 2012 *National Geographic News* reported on a university student who tried to solve this mystery:

> Examining domes on 18 American alligators and 4 Nile crocodiles, [Duncan Leitch] found that the spots contained touch receptors tuned specifically to pressure and vibration, plus a host of raw nerve endings. The domes didn't respond to salt or electricity, but they did *respond* to the touch of von Frey filaments—hairlike, standardized wires used to gauge sensation levels. . . . "My professor and I didn't believe at first that they could be that reactive," Leitch said. "We closed our eyes and tried to tickle each other with [the filaments] on our fingertips, and neither of us could even feel it."

Source: Shannon Fischer. "Croc Jaws More Sensitive than Human Fingertips." National Geographic Daily News. *National Geographic*, November 8, 2012. Web. Accessed March 21, 2013.

Consider Your Audience

Read this passage closely. How would you adapt it for a different audience, such as your classmates, your parents, or younger friends? Write a blog post explaining the information in this passage to the new audience.

CHAPTER FOUR

A WARM HOME

Crocodiles can be found throughout the Western Hemisphere in North America, Central America, and South America. They also live in many regions of the Eastern Hemisphere. Different croc species can be found in Africa, Southeast Asia, and Australia.

As its name suggests, the Australian saltwater crocodile often lives in salt water. It can also live in

Crocodiles live in warm salt water and fresh water around the world.

freshwater areas. Members of this species usually begin their lives in fresh water. But competition for food soon becomes a problem. Older crocs force young adult crocs to move into saltwater areas. Some of these animals remain in the saltier environment. Others move up or down the coast. They try to find new homes near freshwater rivers.

The American crocodile can also be found in both fresh water and brackish water. Brackish water contains more salt than fresh water, but it is not as salty as ocean water. Lakes and rivers make up the American crocs'

A Talented Predator

The slender-snouted crocodile lives in the countries of Central and West Africa. The slender-snouted croc spends more time in water than other species. It can be found in lakes and rivers with dense vegetation cover. The narrow snout of this species gives the animal a special ability. This croc uses its slender snout to grab prey from small underwater holes. The mouth acts almost like a pair of tweezers. It helps the croc snatch fish, shrimp, and crabs from tiny hiding spots.

freshwater homes. A large number of American crocs live in Lago Enriquillo, a lake in the Dominican Republic. This body of water contains an especially high amount of salt for a lake.

Sometimes weather or natural disasters play a part in where a crocodile lives. Most Orinoco crocodiles live in freshwater areas of Colombia and Venezuela. But people have seen this species in the salty waters of Trinidad. This island lies approximately 150 miles (241 km) to the north of Venezuela. Many people think that flooding swept the animals out to sea.

A Grain of Salt

Crocodiles have special glands on their tongues. These glands are the reason crocs can live in salty water. The glands help the crocs remove excess salt from their bodies. This ability may help explain why crocodiles live in so many areas of the world. If food is limited or if competition for food is high in freshwater areas, crocs can move to saltwater areas. They can live in salt water for days or even weeks at a time.

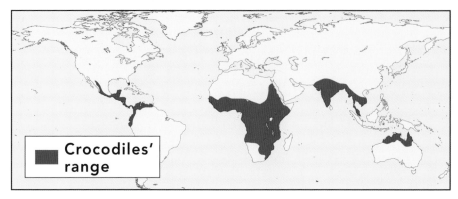

Crocs Around the World
Crocodiles live near warm salt and fresh waters all over the world. This map shows where crocodiles make their homes. Why might crocodiles live in these areas? Write a few sentences describing a crocodile's habitat.

Cold-Blooded Creatures

Whichever parts of the world they call home, all crocs prefer a warm climate. Like other reptiles, crocodiles are cold-blooded animals. They rely on their environments for warmth. Most croc species are most active when the warmest weather arrives.

Many species of crocodile live along grassy swamps and slow-moving rivers. They dig out burrows with their feet and snouts along the water's edge. When the weather is cooler, crocs retreat into these dens. When it gets warmer, they come out to snooze in the sunshine.

Crocodiles keep cool by staying very still during hot weather. This lowers their body temperatures.

Some crocodiles estivate during the dry season. This is similar to hibernation. It is very hot during this time, and the crocs are at risk of overheating. They stay very still and save their energy. The crocs don't eat during this time. They slow down their breathing and their heart rates. This lowers their body temperatures, helping them to stay cool.

CHAPTER FIVE

HUNTER BECOMES THE HUNTED

There are almost no other animals that hunt crocodiles. Some crocodiles eat smaller crocs when the opportunity arises. Every now and then a big cat such as a jaguar or leopard will kill a crocodile. Extremely large snakes such as anacondas and pythons have also been known to eat crocs occasionally. Most animals, however, run from the powerful jaws of this predator.

Crocodiles are some of the top predators in their habitats.

Humans are crocodiles' most dangerous predators. At one time people hunted crocodiles for their hides. Belts, handbags, and boots and shoes made from crocodile skins once sold for extremely high prices. By the 1970s crocodile populations had dropped due to overhunting.

Many people worried that the species might become extinct. Therefore, many countries added crocodiles to their endangered species lists. Hunting crocodiles was outlawed in many parts of the world. But some people ignored the new laws. These people, called poachers, still hunt crocodiles today, even though it is illegal.

Crocodile Farms

Since crocodile hunting has been restricted, crocodile farms have begun popping up all over the world. Six of these farms can be found today in Queensland, Australia, alone. The businesses raise crocs for their meat and skins. They also welcome tourists and other visitors who want to see live crocodiles in action. Most farms make a point of teaching the public about the importance of conservation for wild crocs.

Signs warning humans to stay out of waters known to have crocodiles help prevent crocodile attacks on people.

Crocs and Humans

Croc attacks on humans are rare. But in Australia, many people think they still happen too often. In Australia crocodiles kill an average of two humans each year.

Steve Irwin

In 2006 the world lost one of its biggest crocodile conservationists. His name was Steve Irwin. But he was known to millions of people worldwide as the Crocodile Hunter. Irwin wasn't really a hunter at all. He was the host of a popular television show about crocs and other wild animals. He and his family owned the Australia Zoo. Irwin was killed by a stingray while snorkeling in 2006. His wife Terri and his children, Bindi and Robert, now carry on his important work.

One of the reasons that crocodiles attack humans is habitat encroachment. In many areas people have taken over land that was once used by crocs and other animals. More crocs are forced to live together in smaller areas. They have more competition for food and other resources. Crocs and humans are more likely to run into one another.

Saving Crocodile Species

The International Union for Conservation of Nature (IUCN) keeps track of the most endangered animals in the world. Four crocodile species are on the IUCN's Red List of critically endangered animals. They are the

Steve Irwin was one of the most well-known crocodile conservationists.

Cuban crocodile, the Orinoco crocodile, the Philippine crocodile, and the Siamese crocodile.

Conservation groups work to protect crocodiles from both hunting and habitat encroachment. These groups set aside land for crocodile species. National

Today there are approximately 150,000 saltwater crocs in Australia.

parks and nature preserves provide crocs and other animals with safe places to live. Conservation groups also raise money to send scientists into areas where croc populations are decreasing. The scientists study the crocodiles and their environments in these areas. These scientists hope to find new ways to help the species survive.

EXPLORE ONLINE

The focus of Chapter Five is threats to crocodiles. It also discusses protecting crocodile populations. The Web site at the link below also discusses crocodile conservation. As you know, every source is different. How is the information given on the Web site different from the information in this chapter? How is it the same? What new information can you learn from this Web site?

Conserving Crocodiles
www.mycorelibrary.com/crocodile

Conservation groups also teach people about why it is important to protect crocs. If just one crocodile species becomes extinct, it will affect many other animal species. The populations of the crocodiles' prey may rise. This could throw off the balance of the entire ecosystem.

Crocodiles have been around for millions of years. They play an important role in the food chain. Humans must find a way to protect the crocs' habitat. We need to live peacefully with these important reptiles so they are around for years to come!

Common Name: Crocodile

Scientific Name: *Crocodylus*

Average Size: 5 to 17 feet (1.5–5 m) long; varies greatly among species

Average Weight: 50 to 1,000 pounds (23–450 kg); varies greatly among species

Color: Grayish green or dark brown

Average Lifespan: 30 to 50 years

Diet: Fish, hippos, zebras, dingoes, kangaroos, wallabies, birds, crabs, turtles, and carrion

Habitat: Warm salt and fresh water in North America, Central America, South America, Africa, Southeast Asia, and Australia

Predators: Humans, jaguars, leopards, large snakes, and other crocodiles

Did You Know?

- Crocodiles can live to be 110 years old.
- A rubber band can hold a crocodile's mouth shut.
- A crocodile can survive for an entire year without eating.

Dig Deeper

After reading this book, what questions do you still have about crocodiles? Maybe you want to learn more about their hunting habits or their habitat. Write down one or two questions that can guide you in doing research. With an adult's help, find a few reliable sources that can help answer your questions. Then write a few sentences about how you did your research and what you learned from it.

Why Do I Care?

Whether or not you share a habitat with crocodiles, these reptiles are important predators. How might you be affected if crocodiles were to become extinct? Would other animals that you hardly ever see now become pests due to overpopulation? Make a list of the ways that you and everyone around you might be affected if the American crocodile were to become extinct.

Surprise Me

Learning about new animals can be interesting and surprising. Chapter Two of this book talked about crocodiles' life cycles. What two or three facts about a croc's life cycle did you find most surprising? Why did you find these facts surprising?

Tell the Tale

Write 200 words from the point of view of a crocodile that was forced to leave its home due to habitat encroachment. Make sure to set the scene, develop a sequence of events, and include a conclusion.

GLOSSARY

brackish
partially salty

camouflage
patterns or coloring that help
disguise or hide an animal

carrion
dead and rotting flesh

conservation
management of natural
resources for continued use

ecosystem
the group of plants and
animals living in and
interacting with their
environment

encroachment
when humans move into the
habitat of animals

estivate
to spend a hot, dry season in
an inactive state

extinct
no longer found alive

microchip
a small electronic device that
researchers can use to track
an animal

poacher
someone who collects or
hunts an animal illegally

species
a group of similar animals
that are closely related
enough to mate with one
another

LEARN MORE

Books

Aronsky, Jim. *Crocodile Safari*. New York: Scholastic, 2009.

Hamilton, Sue. *Attacked by a Crocodile*. Edina, MN: ABDO, 2010.

Jagno-Cohen, Judith. *Crocodiles*. Tarrytown, NY: Marshall Cavendish, 2003.

Web Links

To learn more about crocodiles, visit ABDO Publishing Company online at **www.abdopublishing.com**. Web sites about crocodiles are featured on our Book Links page. These links are routinely monitored and updated to provide the most current information available.

Visit **www.mycorelibrary.com** for free additional tools for teachers and students

INDEX

ABOUT THE AUTHOR

Tammy Gagne has written more than 50 books for both adults and children. She resides in northern New England with her husband, son, and a menagerie of animals.